Rhymes & Ructions

Ballads and Banter from Ballyclare

by Jack McKinney

Printed in 2022 by Shanway Press,
15 Crumlin Road, Belfast BT14 6AA

ISBN: 978-1-910044-38-4

Acknowledgements

I would like to thank the following for providing photographs and giving permission to use these in the book and those who supplied stories and background information on the authors of the ballads.

Joanne Boal (née Robinson), Tom Andrew, Rosemary Warwick, (née Scott), Joyce Gray, Matthew Gray, Wilbert Hollinger, Jack Gowdy and Wilson Logan.

I'd also thank Leila and Zoe McKinney, for their drawing and story about the Aliens Landing in Doagh, and Joan McKinney, whose patience and general assistance proved indispensable.

Introduction

The title of this book needs some explanation. Rhymes and Ructions refers to the title of a series of concerts organised by the Ballyclare and District Historical Society in Ballyclare in the late 1970s and early 1980s. These comprised music, songs and recitations performed by groups and local entertainers in traditional, informal style. They gradually gained popularity with the audience and, being held on the Monday night before the annual May Fair Day, reflected the atmosphere of jollification that pervaded the town at this special time of year.

The music was provided by various groups of instrumentalists – fiddlers, accordionists, tin whistle players – and their sessions were interspersed with songs, recitations and stories by local individual entertainers drawn from the lore and culture of the Six Mile Water region. Many of these songs and much of the material came from an oral tradition and few were available in written form.

Sadly the concerts came to an end when the security situation dictated that crowds gathering in halls became impossible. The Historical Society planned to celebrate the 40th anniversary of the founding of the society in 1980 by reviving the Rhymes and Ructions concert in 2020 but the outbreak of the Covid-19 pandemic put paid to their plans.

What I have endeavoured to do is compile a collection of the ballads and anecdotes that proved so popular at the concerts. The tone and subjects of the ballads vary considerably from the amusing to those of a more contemplative nature. As for their credibility I leave the readers to assess this for themselves. I must emphasise, though, that while the unexpected arrival of Aliens in Doagh and the shipwreck on the Six Mile Water may seem preposterous, a couple of others, that may appear ridiculous including the installation of a Superloo in Ballyclare Square, are essentially based on real events!

A word about the language used in the book. The ballads are recorded in the style and language used in the originals – standard English or Ulster-Scots. The stories and other text may contain either or both. I have often followed the style of a mixture of Ulster -Scots and English as in the Scottish 'Kaleyard' novels, familiar to readers of Archibald McIlroy's books, where the conversational dialogue of characters is in Ulster-Scots with the rest of the narrative in standard English.

Whatever your taste in Literature or Fantasy I do hope that you enjoy the ballads and banter in the following pages.

Jack McKinney

Contents

Contents

The Six Mile Water at Ballyclare

The Six Mile Water

From the scree slopes up above on Shane's dark brooding hill
To the little wandering stream below where cattle drink their fill,
Here springs the lovely river once known as Owen-na-view,
But is now the Six Mile Water, banks glistening in the dew.

As it runs right down the valley where the gleaming pebbles ring,
It's the purest ever, supplied not by what men bring.
From the Park Moss up in 'Boley it's small to Ballynure,
But there two rivers join it – of a welcome it is sure.

The Bryantang and the Castle burns come tumbling further on,
Where four townlands for long have met, they sing a merry song.
They pick the Six Mile up in spate, the Stick-Brig flows below
It's now a lovely river, on its banks the cattle grow.

Through Dunturkey on to Skilgan through fields
    both ploughed and not,
It flows right down through Ballyclare,
    past the ancient Norman Motte.
It winds its way through pastures green, but progress now is slow
For many a dark pool lies in shade where the big fish always go.

Slow flowing toward the pillar tower in lovely Antrim town
It wends its stately way 'tween banks as soft as thistle down;
In majestic flow down through the vale it lifts its head sublime,
That fine old stately river, that conqueror of time.

It passes not a Roman arch or temple of the Greek,
It flows near sweet Rathmore where the kings of old grew weak,
It wends its way through townlands fair,
    names vanished in the gloom,
Forgotten as the strife of men, or body in the tomb.

As plundering Norsemen filled the Vale,
    dark shadows did they cast;
From Olderfleet they spread around and from the Bann at last
Unruffled yet by men's dark deeds its stately banks adorn;
Serene and calm it gently flows for generations yet unborn.

To you, my lovely river, your praise I'll always sing
Along your banks good men were reared in shadow of thy wing;
The travelling man with rapture can, no matter where he goes
Look back with grace, with smile on face,
    where the Six Mile Water flows.

Ernest McA Scott

Ernie Scott enjoyed a long life in Straid, Ballynure and Ballyclare as a farmer, garage owner, lorry driver and part-time soldier. He always had an abiding interest in the history and culture of his beloved Six Mile Water district. His knowledge included not only the basic historical background of the villages where he lived but the local and national issues affecting the lives and customs of the people of the area. The books he compiled on Straid and Ballynure late on in his life bear testimony to such knowledge and his scholarship.

He was a founder member of the Ulster-Scots Language Society and was active in several local historical societies including those in Carrickfergus and Ballyclare.

However many folk consider that Ernie's best talent lay in giving amusing and informative talks to a range of audiences spread across Ulster. These were never dull and often covered a description of a variety of characters he had met in the course of his social and working life and anecdotes they had recounted.

He was a prolific composer of verses and his subjects ranged from the humorous to the lyrical. His command of the Ulster-Scots language was especially impressive. Each summer he was invited to attend an annual meeting of eminent Ulster poets in Islandmagee. He had become their authority on the correct pronunciation of the Ulster-Scots language in the poetry of those usually known as The Weaver Poets of the late 18th and early 19th centuries. I am confident that in the evening sessions he would have been persuaded by his distinguished audience to recite one or two of his own ballads and entertain them with some of his stories and anecdotes.

Ernie Scott in his favourite seat

Ernie's Stories

Willie was a pensioner resident in Ballynure. Well known in the area he drove an old fashioned Morris Minor car, rather indifferently at times. He wore thick – lensed spectacles and as he drove around the district his little Jack Russell terrier was to be seen seated happily in the front passenger seat. Folk said that this was Willie's guide dog. Not too many locals were tempted to accompany him on his travels around the district but on one occasion a friend accepted a lift from Ballyclare to Ballynure in the Morris Minor. Travelling at his usual sedate pace along the busy Templepatrick Road he approached the turn off for Ballynure. Heading for the Morris Minor at speed was a 40ft truck coming from the port at Larne. Engaged in conversation with his passenger Willie made a sudden abrupt turn across the carriageway. The driver of the truck, appalled at this manoeuvre, braked sharply while leaning heavily on his horn. As the rear end of the Morris Minor just made it into Ballynure Willie remarked quite nonchalantly to his terrified passenger. 'Now, there you are – everybody knows me!'

A widow lived frugally in a small holding on the outskirts of Ballynure. In her lonely life two animals were her pride and joy – a large tortoiseshell cat and a calf she reared up over the summer to sell in Ballyclare market at the hind end of the year. She noticed one day that the cat seemed a bit off colour and was not using the litter tray regularly – it was, in the common parlance, 'tinged up'. She persuaded a local lad to cycle into Ballyclare to fetch a dose for the distressed animal. He set off on his bike but on the way fell in with some friends in Millvale. When he proceeded on his journey and reached the vet's premises he had forgotten whether the dose was for the cat or the calf. He took a chance and asked for a dose for a calf. Although it seemed a large bottle for a cat, the widow duly gave it to the cat over the next few days. About a week later Dr Logan, the vet, was on a call in the area and called with the widow. He asked how her calf was progressing. He was surprised to hear that it was the cat that needed the dose. 'Don't tell me that you gave the whole bottle to the cat! I must see this cat,' he declared. She led him over to the window from which he could see seven cats at the bottom of the garden. 'I can see your tortoiseshell cat in the middle of that melee but what are the other six doing?'

'Well,' said the widow, 'there are two scraping, two covering and two looking for fresh ground.'

Ernie attended a funeral in Ballynure one afternoon and later in the evening having refreshment in Ballyclare he met a friend. 'Do you know where I was this afternoon?' he remarked. 'No' said the friend. 'I was at Sammy Davison's funeral,' replied Ernie. 'Och, Big Sammy's not dead, is he?' said the friend? 'Well, if he is not,' said Ernie, 'we played a very dirty trick on him this afternoon!'

A well known 'druth' often had rather too much to drink in The Ballad Inn in Ballynure. His usual, unsteady way home led across the cemetery. One night on his way home he stumbled into an open grave that had been prepared for a funeral there the next day. Too far gone to scramble out he settled down and his deep slumber was only interrupted by the six o'clock horn from the Whitepark Mill across the Six Mile Water. Groggily he scratched his way to the edge of the grave and had a sleepy look around the deserted cemetery. Said he to himself, 'Man dear – The Last Trump and it's a danged bad turn – out from Ballynure!'

Falling into open graves in Ballynure cemetery apparently was far from a rare occurrence. Another drunk interred in this way woke up the next morning shouting 'Oh it's coul I declare I am foundered!' Hearing the shouts the gravedigger approached, saw the predicament and remarked, 'Man dear, it's nae wonder, ye have scraped all the moul aff yersel.'

In days gone by the minister in Ballynure Presbyterian Church existed on a very meagre stipend and was forced to be careful to afford the necessities of life in the manse. He did employ an old chap who tended the manse garden with what could only be described as very ancient tools. One afternoon the pair of hedge shears he was struggling with came apart in his hands. Warily he knocked the door of the manse and did his best to explain that the disaster of the broken shears was no fault of his and caused by the age and condition of the implement. His Reverence listened to his explanation then curtly replied, 'Evidently, Samuel, evidently.' Samuel was rather confused by the remark and later asked a friend, 'What did his reverence mean by Evidently?' 'Well, Sam,' said the friend 'do you not realise that this is a clergyman's way of saying you are a bloomin' liar!'

At one time during his part-time military career Ernie grew a large handlebar moustache. He was due to meet a person on historical society business in the Square in Ballyclare. They had never met before and the fellow asked Ernie how he might recognise him in this busy location.

'Oh' said Ernie, 'just look out for a tallish chap with a face like a burst horsehair sofa.'

The Wreck of the Never–Budge

Times are hard, aye, very hard,
And Billy's hard to please.
Young Sammy has made up his mind
That he will cross the seas.

There were men on board of every trade,
All from the shamrock shore,
Preachers and law doctors
And gluttons by the score.

Sammy Love from Ballycorr,
Bob Doherty and Jack.
And William John O'Hara
From a place called Tannybrack.

They left the port of Ballycorr
Just by the break of day
And down the Six Mile Water,
The vessel steered her way.

Poor Jack Carmichael bathed in tears,
Upon the deck did stand,
And sighed for the girl he left behind,
In his own native land.

When they came to Ballyclare,
A dreadful storm came on;
The captain says 'My jolly lads,
I fear we are all done.

O'Hara then aloud did pray
That spared thy all might be,
And spoke of him who stilled the waves
On the lake of Galilee

The captain and the gallant crew
Did work with might and will
'Twas all in vain, she struck a rock
Down by the Paper Mill.

And when she stuck upon the rock,
'Twas dreadful for to hear
The cries of those poor emigrants
Would have almost rent your ear.

To the bottom went the Never–Budge,
A melancholy wreck
In a watery grave lie Sammy Love,
O'Hara, Bob and Jack.

John Reid, Whitepark

The Smithy, Ballynure

Heard at the Six Mile Bridge on Main Street

Before the Narrow Gauge Railway came through Ballyclare a favourite place for men in the evening was around the Main Street Bridge. Many were the topics discussed and stories recounted as they leaned over the railing, every now and again spitting tobacco juice into the Six Mile River. One night they got on to the subject of Physics. One old fellow addressed his friend, 'Tam, they say that if ye thraw a stane up in the air, it's the force o' grevity that brings her doon.'

'Weel Sam, I think she'll com doon onyway, nivver min' yer grevity!'

One other evening the two friends watched as a small early- type biplane made its slow and steady progress across the horizon. Said Wull,

'Tam, I wouldnae like tae be up there in that thing!'
'Weel min' you, Wull, I wouldnae like tae be up there wi'oot it !'

The conversation often turned to fishing in the Six Mile River and, typically with fishermen, exaggeration of the size of the fish to be found there. Sam boasted, 'M' da told me that he had once caught a big trout and it measured a foot – between the eyes!'

'Listen, Sam,' broke in Wull, 'the biggest fish ever seen in that river was a powerful length. Its tail was under the Six Mile bridge in Ballyclare and its heid was worrying sheep on Ballyboley hill. Now beat that if you can!'

Lines on the Ballynure Ball

Another grand event is past,
And one that crowns them all.
It was published by invitation
As a social and a ball.

The event took place in Ballynure
And was a great success.
It was held in a spacious granary
Lent by the Lady Mayoress.

The invitations were given out
To every swank and snob ;
The ladies' fare was sandwiches,
The gentlemen's two bob.

The committee they were all high class,
As everybody knows;
But some of them could not appear
Because they had no clothes.

The ladies came from far and near
From Straid and Ballygowan,
And some of them from Ballycorr,
And some from the Paper Town.

The gentlemen came tripping in
With overcoats galore.
But some of them were awful sights
Upon a dancing floor!

They opened the ball in ancient form
It was a treat you're sure,
To see them prancing round the ring,
Those heroes from Ballynure.

It was brother Scott that led in song,
And he's the boy can sing,
When he gets in a stout or two
He can make the rafters ring.

The gentlemen were not polite
And that is one thing sure,
But you couldn't expect much better
From a crowd in Ballynure !

They ran the ball till six o' clock
And then the fun did end ;
So every young man in the room
Looked for a lady friend.

This rambling statement now must close
Before the clock strikes ten
I'll raise my glass and drink good health
To the members of 610.

Anon

On James Campbell – the celebrated poet of Ballynure

Where Nature's flowers faintly bloom,
Poor Campbell lived in cot obscure,
Yet genius found him on the loom,
Upon the wild and barren moor,
His was no muse that praised the great,
Or turned his lyre for selfish ends,
He sung to soothe his destined fate,
He sung to please his bosom friends.

Anon

The Bard of Ballynure was a well known local Mason and wrote a poem entitled 'Address to the Masonic Brethren of Ballyeaston 725,' which described his entry into freemasonry.

Some of the lines ran:

…. The Masonic sons of Ballyeaston ,
may their actions ever shine bright;
Them chiefly I laid my request on,
to bring me from darkness to light.
They taught me to work in their temple,
The highest cupola to crown;
They knew they could get the example
I ne'er staggered my brain to look down.

They taught me the use of dividers,
the sectors, the square and the gauge,
the level, the plumb – rule and mallet
the lever, the screw and the wedge;
The use of large butments and levels

to use step by step with a grace.
They showed me the square of the ladder
was equal to upright and base.

James Campbell
Songs and Poems published in 1870 by Samuel Corry
Ballyclare

The Old School

As I was walking up the road,
And on to Skilganaban,
I saw the ruins of the old schoolhouse
Where I my studies began.

What memories came across my mind
Of days long since gone by
Of playmates, scattered here and there,
I thought of them with a sigh.

The one – roomed school, with the desks well worn,
The maps that hung on the wall.
The old – fashioned shelves where we stored our books,
And the big square tiles in the hall.

No running water to wash our hands,
But an odd - looking stand was there,
With a basin on top and a jug beneath
Which we filled from the stream with care.

The strong, solid door bore the marks of time,
Broken windows and shutters hung loose ;
The steps well- worn with many feet,
The walls showing signs of abuse.

I thought of the old schoolmaster so fierce,
Who shouted, ranted and raved.
He flailed the lazy ones on with a stick
The clever ones usually were saved.

He had piercing eyes that missed not a thing,
A hand that was quick on the draw.
If you didn't come fast when he called your name
You were likely to have a sore jaw.

Oh where are the Kennedys, Finlays and Hills
McMeekins - to name but a few?
Alas, some have passed on and some have gone
To dwell in pastures new.

In times good and bad, what fun we had
As we learned the golden rule.
The ones that are left, I'm sure will spare
A thought for that dear old school.

Elizabeth Workman

*Elizabeth Workman lived in Millvale
and had a strong connection with Ballyclare Presbyterian
Church where she was a long standing member of the choir.*

Ball'easton School

Ball'easton – how quiet you've grown through the day,
Since the wains from the village have all gone away
To learn their school lessons in far away places,
No more will we see their happy wee faces.

For the school on the hill stands silent and shut,
And the desks are away where once the wains sut.
No more will the bell ring around nine o'clock,
When the village schoolmaster would summon his flock.

Now how could this happen, you well may enquire
For surely this village a school should require ;
I'm told it's entirely the work of a fool
Who deprived us all of a shining new school.

A few years ago, the story began,
When Stormont decided to study a plan
To build a new school all gleaming and white,
But they couldn't agree on a choice of a site.

They argued for months on where it should be,
And even turned down a fine site that was free.
But the head man from Stormont never would yield,
He wanted it built next to Sam Agnew's field

The name of this man, I'm afraid I can't mention,
But his choice of a site was beyond comprehension;
He may have been smart but his gumption was hidden
To contemplate building so near to a midden!

Now the Ministry man was a law to himself,
So the plans were withdrawn and put on the shelf.
He packed up his bags and went back to Belfast,
And the new school became a dream of the past.

But worse was to come, the school roll declined,
New pupils were getting much harder to find,
A letter arrived to add to our woes
'It has been decided your school has to close.'

And so fate had played a mean, heinous trick
For there we were dreaming of rows of new brick,
But our dreams fell around us before they'd begun
Instead of a new school, now we had none.

Take warning wee schools in valley and glen,
Beware of the visits of Ministry men!
They'll promise the moon and tell you more lies,
Then close down your school in front of your eyes.

George Cochrane

In 1980 a new school to cater for children from Ballyclare and Ballyeaston opened in Hillmount Avenue, Ballyclare. It was named Fairview Primary School.

The Auld Wife's Lament to her Spinning Wheel

Frae Tibbie Gordon I gat this wheel,
An' then I was young, an' my face was fair,
An' since the first day, she cam into my **shiel,**
We aye had something to keep an' to spare
On the wintry night by the clear ingle side
My wee bit lamp hung laigh in the **lum**;
An I sung my sang, an' my wheel I plied,
An Rorie was pleased wi' the hartsome hum.
But now upon her I maun spin nae mair,
An' it mak's my heart both sorry an' sair.

Now fare thee weel, my cantie wee wheel,
In age an' youth my staff an' my stay,
How gladly at gloamin' my kind auld chiel
Has reeled our pirn, sae bonnie an' blae
But men o' cunning, an **pelf**, an' pride,
Hae made thee a useless thing to me;
For they care na what puir bodies betide,
Or whether they live on the yirth or die.
Now the **feck** o' my fare is a heart fu' o' wae
An' the fourth o' a groat is the wage o' a day.

Thomas Beggs

Thomas Beggs was a highly regarded poet of the group often called the Rhyming Weavers. Beggs, though, was a bleacher at Mallusk and Ballyclare. He travelled around a lot before succumbing to typhus in 1847. Editions of his verse were printed by Samuel Corry of Ballyclare.

shiel – cabin or hut; **pelf** – wealth
lum – chimney; **feck** – portion

Matt's Song

Ballyboley is a spot that's known near and far,
There's a boy up in this district that drives a wedding car,
He's jolly and light-hearted I hear the people say,
And when he takes you for a run he isn't hard to pay.

He is a skilful driver and never does things rash,
He has been driving cars for years and never had a crash,
So now I give his name to you , to spell it isn't hard
His address is Ballyboley and his name is Matt Meharg.

And there he lives quite happily close by to Ballynure
So I'd advise you on your wedding day to get him and make
sure,
And he will take you to the church and away round the foam,
And when your day is over he will bring you safely home.

And then your life will sweetly start and end so sweetly far,
And I wish you all great happiness when in his wedding car.

Poetical tribute from a satisfied customer
of Meharg's Taxi Service

Matt Meharg, A Gentleman of Song

From an Article in East Antrim Times
18th February 1981, by Judith Watson

Matt Meharg is a born story teller. He is one of a dying breed of
folk singers, has lived for all but two years of his life in the same
country house, yet his reputation stretches the length and breadth
of County Antrim and beyond.

Well known as a partner in the Meharg Brothers garage in Ballyboley which is as much a landmark as the townland of Ballyboley itself. He once earned his living as a taxi driver in the district and many a tale is told of how he used to entertain customers with a song or two, notably when rushing to get a bride to the church in time. At one time he had a regular booking to take young folk, and some not so young, to the Saturday dances in the famous Rinkha ballroom in Islandmagee. He remembers with amusement one particular occasion when he was asked to sing at a concert, at which a well – known choir was also to perform. The choir members arrived with large bundles of manuscript tucked under their arms and Matt, standing with his hands in his pockets, was asked where his music was. The white-haired Matt tapped his head in reply: 'It's in here,' he said. Matt is one of those rare people who sing what the late Sam Henry from Coleraine called 'Songs of the People' songs written by ordinary folk about people who lived in centuries long past. Matt attended regular Music Festivals. On the subject of these competitions one of Mr Meharg's favourite stories is about a man who went to a local competition and when asked by the piano accompanist which key he wanted his song played in, he looked blankly and shrugged his shoulders in confusion. 'What note do you want then?' came the next question to which the puzzled man replied, 'I don't know.' Then with a sudden understanding, he reached into his inside pocket and produced a piece of string which he carefully laid across the piano keyboard.

'That's the note I want,' he declared, pointing to the upper end.

'I think I would need a piece of string, too' admits Matt with a laugh.

Matt Meharg and his treasured Penny Farthing bicycle

The Ballycarry Bachelor

I might have married when I was young,
but I was hard to please.
Marryin' kinda scared me, the more I liked a squeeze.
I asked a friend's advice, he said – you may either do or don't,
You'll be sorry if you marry and you'll be sorry if you won't.

Now though on the business of marriage I had been fully bent,
His wise words gave me bother,and I wasn't just content,
As I tried to find an answer I got tied into a knot,
Whiles I thought I thought I would marry
and whiles I thought, maybe not!

But just to keep my spirits up I had an odd 'kerfuffle,'
And whiles I got a cuff or two when this led to a scuffle .
So life went on from day to day and years wore on by degrees,
Till I wasn't fit or active enough to cope with all the sprees.

Then my life got very lonely since I made my big mistake,
And I found it didn't suit me when I had to learn to bake,
I longed for some companion just to brighten up my life.
Till one day I determined that I would find a wife.

Now Mary was the sweetest thing – a beauty in her day,
So I thought I would approach her and hear what she would say.
But her answer to my question made me very far from proud,
I got two clouts from the poker and her shouts were more than loud.

I never ran as fast before, folk thought I had the **scar** ,
I passed a bus goin' up to Larne and a private motor car,
I made for Ballycarry, doing all was in my power
I flew round the Rinkha Corner at fifty miles an hour!

So my marrying days are over and I just must settle down,
I come in every Friday for my pension to the town.
If I had been a wise man I could have had a wife
But now I'm just an old **gurn** and a bachelor for life.

Anon; Song from Matt's extensive repertoire

Those listening to this piece and, knowing Matt's reputation as a confirmed bachelor, must have been tempted to alter the title to The Ballyboley Bachelor.

scar (or scoor) – an Ulster word for a common affliction of cattle, producing very frequent and loose motions, in humans termed diahorrea, sometimes in country-speak called 'the backdoor trot.'

gurn – a person given to excess and scathing complaining, often with no reasonable cause.

The Thatch Cottage

The Thatch

*Written as a lament for the old inn known as The Thatch on Main
Street Ballyclare and demolished to make room for The Ulster Bank.*

Old Ballyclare of sweet renown,
Will soon be just a modern Town.
For year by year you've seen no doubt
Its ancient homesteads passing out.

And now at last wae grief and pain
I see 'The Thatch' has just been slain.
That dear old hoose 'o' memory sweet
Has disappeared clean off our street.

Each stone and stick, each straw and rod
Now lie upon old nature's sod
No more we'll meet to quench oor thirst
Or 'toss the coin' for who stands first.

To me it seems a desecration,
A loss to us and all the nation.
But in its place, no doubt, will rise
A building of gigantic size,
A house of strength, a house of rank,
Another blinking Ulster Bank.

Frank Blair
with his
melodian in
The Ballyclare
Minstrel
Troupe

Frank Blair

Frank Blair was a talented Ballyclare entertainer who moulded his stage character on Harry Lauder, the Scots comedian. He often dressed on stage in kilt and sporran. During the First World War he joined the divisional concert party The Merry Mauves and was a distinct success. He tried the professional stage after the war but soon tired of the constant travelling. He returned to Ballyclare to manage the local cinema. He eventually emigrated to America. A farewell concert party was held in his honour in the Ballyclare cinema on 28th November 1930 when he gave a final performance of his usual recitations including The Thatch and Poor Merriet Men and told his popular yarns.

One of these featured an old man on his death bed with his wife sorrowing in silence beside the bed. A weak voice trembled from the bed, 'Maggie, I think I am about to go on a long, long journey.' Between loud sobs Maggie managed a mumbled reply, 'Weel, John, you'll aye hae yin consolation. It'll be all doon the hill, all doon the hill!

Poor Merriet Men

Hae pity freens and a wee kind word
For those who've lost their freedom,
And dinna harden up yer hearts,
When we go on the Spreedom.

But through it a' remember that
Oor sufferings are sincere,
And that is why indeed, dear freens,
We go upon the beer.

A merriet man has ups and doons
Which always keeps him guessin',
Nae matter what he tries tae dae,
The wife aye says he's messin'.

And women can make life hell,
Altho' we call them jewels,
And smile on them frae day to day,
As they dish up oor gruels.

We hear that Adam lost his job,
When in the dear old garden,
Through letting Eve influence him,
Which was an awful hard – un.

From then till now it's been the same
And woman's full of evil.
And in her heart as large as life,
There reigns the dear old devil.

And so it is, as through this world
She holds man by the whiskers,
And never lets him free ava
Because ye see – she's mistress.

We read that woman from man's rib,
Was made a living being,
And from that day on, up tae noo,
Poor man has aye been deein'.

Frank Blair

Courting and Some Possible Consequences
The Rolway Lane

I'm just a crazy countryman, fae up amang the hills',
Wi' ne'er a chance to share romance, or love's exciting thrills,
It seems my pals could aye get dolls, but I had never nane,
Till oot I stole an' took a stroll alang the Rolway Lane.

Beside a stile I stops a while and lo it came to pass,
My heart was captivated by a bonnie black – haired lass,
Of coorse I knew her lang ago when she was just a wain,
When it used to be the Railway line instead of Rolway lane.

But noo she's big an' beautiful, her heart is light an' free,
She has nae fau't or ocht like that, except goin' oot wi' me
I know I'm rough and raw enough, the coortin's coorse an' plain,
Still many a girl enjoys a birl alang the Rolway Lane.

As long as providence permits, I'll see her yince a week,
To feel her arm aroon m' neck, her chin against m' cheek
Let rain or hail, or storms prevail, she never waits in vain,
For I would hate tae miss a date alang the Rolway Lane.

A place like this for mortal bliss, nae novel'st could invent,
Like the banks an' brigs an' cabbages rigs that often we frequent,
Withoot her noo, in soul it's true, m' heart would break in twain,
But she cannie stay and leeve her day alang the Rolway Lane.

She'll want a man that's mair refined,an' better dressed than me,
Perhaps some city Romeo wi' lots of L.S.D.
Then fu'-o'-grief, I'll seek relief amang the hills again,
And there lament the nights I spent alang the Rolway lane.

Sandy Robinson

In days gone by there were no fancy cosmetics for simple country women folk to plaster on their faces. Young girls getting dressed up for a date often had to resort to a sprinkle of ordinary flour to dust on to their faces as powder. Some did go a bit heavy on the flour at times. One chap arriving at the front door to escort his date to a dance was a bit overcome with his lady friend's appearance. He described his experience to a friend, ' I knocked the front door, it opened a little bit and her face peeped out. Do you know it was just like a moose luking oot o' a flour beg!'

* * *

A farmer and his wife had a plain, middle-aged daughter whom they feared had missed her 'marriage market.' They were anxious to see her off their hands and were delighted when an eligible bachelor began to take an interest in the daughter. They were pleased to see that their parlour soon became a regular Sunday night 'love nest' and awaited progress with interest. One Sunday night they wondered how the couple were getting on so the wife suggested that she would make a cup of tea and her husband could take it in and report on developments. This he did and coming back out of the parlour with the tea tray he dejectedly said to his wife.' 'Would you believe it?, there they are sitting on two separate chairs singing hymns. Maggie, when you and I were doing our courting the only noise that could be heard from the sofa was the snappin' o' garters!'

* * *

The usual group of idle menfolk were gathered outside John Baird's Inn on Main Street Ballyclare one evening when a motor car drew up beside them. The driver wound down his window and shouted out to the curious ensemble. 'Are any of you fellows familiar with the Doagh turn off?' A down-at-heel chap in a shabby coat stepped forward and addressed the driver 'I think I am, your reverence – I married her!'

The Green Galoot

Before I joined the Young Farmers' Club I wasnae aften oot,
A simple explanation – I was just a big galoot.
Leevin' up in the wilderness where ye nivver hear a joke,
It maks ye feel unaisy when mixin' wi' ither folk.

But time maks alterations and it's very, very strange,
Just let oot the worst galoot and ye'll see the way they'll change.
So I hae altered greatly since the time I joined them first,
I like the lasses noo – the things that scared me worst.

I'd aften heerd o'coortin but nivver got the taste
Till yin night o' a meetin' I asked one and she faced.
I knowed she'd been courted afore and I judged that she'd be tame,
So I put me airm aroon her and I arted her fer hame.

We talked aboot the weather, the craps,
                              the price o' turkeys an' things like that.
But I just hadnae the courage t'ask the lass tae stap!
And as time was fast progressin' an' her hame was drawin' near,
I got mare or less excited an says I, it's either noo or ne'er.

So I walked up close beside her, it was just fernest a bush,
I put m'toe oot in front o' her an' geen her a wee push,
Weel she geen a splatter like somethin' goin' tae faint,
An' her toe cleeked m' trousers and I'm danged but doon she went.

I looked at her a minute fer I thought that she'd be cross,
Sure she said she was expectin' it – but no sae big a toss!
Weel I cuddled her an' I kissed her an' she didnae want tae lee,
Then I asked her if she liked me an 'I think I do says she!'

So all you boys that's nervous it's no sae very hard,
Especially when ye're dealin' wi' the women frae Tildarg!
But here – I can say nae mare aboot it, I'd better drap the matter,
For there may be neighbours readin' this
                              an the less they know the better!

Alex McAllister

Alex McAllister was a rhymester and a performer without equal in East Antrim. He was at his peak during the period 1950-1970 appearing at traditional concerts, reciting his verses, telling yarns and delighting audiences who were often left helpless with laughter.

He was an enthusiastic contributor at functions organised by the Larne and District Folklore Society and complemented a talented group of office bearers of the society in this period, arranging social evenings and producing the society's popular magazine The Corran. This publication enjoyed wide circulation throughout East Antrim and over the years printed many of Alex's ballads and verses.

Many artists nowadays present his material at functions and on air but most people who had heard him perform in person would accept that he was the master of their performance.

He also had a good line in telling amusing, if somewhat incredible, anecdotes and his lively style added to an obvious enthusiasm to perform on a public stage.

Sadly, although his verses remain accessible in print, most of his humorous stories have been lost to posterity. A couple do still exist in the memories of a few of those who heard Alex perform on stage some years ago.

A few examples:
In the early years of rail travel, Maggie and Harry, an aged couple from the remote Carnalbanagh district, made the adventurous trip by train from Larne to Belfast for a day out to see the sights of the big city. At this time the York Street Midland Railway Company terminus had a grand, glass roof and the station complex housed

many shops trading with the arriving and departing throng of passengers. Harry stepped off the train and looking up at the elaborate roof and the bustling shops remarked,

'You know, Maggie if I had known Belfast had had a roof I would not have brought my topcoat!'

The couple ventured outside the station and there Harry spied a carter endeavouring to slip a nosebag with oats over the ears of the horse while he made a delivery – a common sight in the city at this time. Harry studied the operation for a minute then shouted over to the carter, 'Hey boy, you'll never get that big horse into that wee bag!'

Further on towards the city centre they were intrigued by the electric tramcars they saw swinging noisily along the street. They bravely wanted to take a ride but were reluctant to board these dangerous vehicles. As the tramcar stopped, Maggie approached the conductor leaning outside the entrance and asked him, 'Tell me, if I put my foot on one of those gleaming rails would I be electrocuted?'

'No, Madam, 'he assured her, 'not unless you put your other foot up on to the wire!'

Alfie McClean

Alfie McClean started work as a soaper in a barber's shop on Main Street Ballyclare. His job was to do the rounds lathering with his wobbler brush those waiting to be shaved. Many of the customers were farmers from the market having a shave while they were in town with their animals. While waiting they chatted and chewed tobacco and were often not too careful where they spat out the juice, mostly on the earthen floor. A campaign was begun to stop this filthy habit and spitoons were placed strategically around the floor. Alfie was instructed to push these vessels towards the worst offenders with his toe! One old fellow watching what he was about complained to Alfie, 'Luksay, young fellow, if ye dinnae watch oot, I'll spit in that thing!

Herbie and Jimmy Boyd in their barber's shop on Main Street, Ballyclare. Spitoons had gone out of use by the 1950s

Extract from Ye Old Ballyclarians

.... As I dandered down the dusty street
One lovely summer night,
I met a man with countenance rare
Dressed in heavenly white.

He took me gently by the hand,
Be not afraid he said
I am going to speak of those good folk
Who now long since are dead.

Saurday night at the top of the Square,
The Salvation Army would meet ;
Johnnie Barton would preach and sing
With a voice clear and sweet.

In Mary Price's eating house,
Farmers swore by troth
You could travel the whole of Ireland,
And you wouldn't taste better broth.

Billposter, Sam Judy McClean
Would ring his bell and wail,
In John McClelland's auction rooms
Good furniture was for sale.

There were many other jobs,
Billposter Sam would do
Like clean out your midden,
For a silver bob or two.

Houston Craig owned the pub
Well known as The Thatch,
And in his spare time he would fish
And boast about his catch.

Butcher Griffin, barber Dolan
And nailer, Charlie Cole,
And across the street lived cobbler Moore,
Who could mend a broken sole.

William, Thomas and Alex Graham
Were butchers of renown,
Who with their thrift and ability,
Helped to build this town.

Big Mag Allen with her basket of lace,
Red flannel and linens fine
Would often boast of her daily help –
A glass of rhubarb wine.

Keyhole Cunningham and Dummy Harper,
Joe Meeke and Wull McGaw;
Not forgetting the fighting pair,
Bob Johnston and Tackaraa.

Tom McNeilly would laugh and sing,
As he watered the dusty street.
And the boys and girls would run behind
To cool and wash their feet.

The weekly market was a sight
And pigs in every cart,
Were lined across the Doagh Road,
Past the Church of the Sacred Heart.

Tom McKnight the Weigh Master
Would ring the starting bell,
And farmers rushed to get a place
Their produce for to sell.

'Hind door off, the kerb stane watch
How many have you got?
Pull them off, keep the straw
You're sure that is the lot?

Sam McKissock, auld John Grange,
John Erskine and Wille Hugh
Sold wines and spirits of every sort,
And also mountain dew..........

Alfie McClean

And on and on it goes, for up to 100 verses more!

The Stranger's Return to Ballyclare (1884)

O home of my youth and younger days,
What changes time brings, the stranger says;
As he looks where once was the Fair Green,
A bright new row of shops is seen,
And the opposite side you wouldn't know,
For when I was young it was old Pound Row,
The monument stands to the old doctor's fame –
A landmark, and a mark to the noble name.

A railway is running into town, I'm telling true –
A narrow gauge line to Larne and Ballymena new;
The station stands where Tom Houston used to dye –
The route takes the meadows, the Six Mile close by,
And the Northern Counties is coming right in –
At the foot of the town will be heard the din –
Where John McDowell used to live in times long ago,
There the station is built, there the engine will blow.

Nimmon's Row has undergone great changes,
Shops and buildings now along it ranges;
William Lawson is no more at the old stand, I declare
He's gone to a higher place above (in Ballyclare!)
James Milliken looks youthful and lives as of old;
William lives private or at least so I am told;
Mr Hill has got married and looks very trim;
But no youth in his orchard will want to see him.

Sam Moore is no younger, but stands his age well,
With a little of the Native will join, buy, or sell ;
The rim of the hat just shading the eye,
Sam will pull down his vest, and look rather shy;
Weel, weel, no man it was a *weethin'* footy
Aboot the toon parks and the landlord booty;
William, although older, looks younger than Sam,
And a great grandfather is by the eldest Tam.

Anon, 1884

The above verses in a discoloured folder were discovered in a box of mixed rubbish before being left out for the bin collection and offered to the author in case the parcel might contain interesting articles. Other items included a child's work book used in Ballyclare Boys' National School in 1875 and an early copy of the Boys Own comic paper. The Resident's Return forms an interesting comparison with Alfie McClean's descriptions of shopkeepers and characters in Ballyclare in the first half of the 20th century.

Sweet Ballyclare – Where they Keep no Sunday!*

Come let us weigh the balance fair,
And see what's wrong with Ballyclare,
That it should bear a foul disgrace,
To talk about in every place.

Now he who would the plummet lay,
If by himself the balance weigh,
Must show to all his beam is true
Or else his judgement will not do.

But since the balance's all astray,
We now must try some other way,
And take the whole and then compare,
To find what's wrong with Ballyclare.

But let us always bear in mind,
We have to deal with human kind;
And balance all that's frail or true,
For some are right as well as you.

For the Grundy family isn't dead,
As they can live on fancied bread;
And 'straight' their neighbours one and all,
Though they themselves are not so tall.

They rail on customs every day,
And cry the world is gone astray;
They only wish they had the tawse,
They'd scourge the boys for broken laws.

If fashion's boots have narrow toes,
And you take fashion as it goes,
Don't blame the fashion, if you please,
Blame pride that will not give you ease.

But rail they will without a cause,
And think they could amend the laws,
They cry the church is gone astray,
Because they cannot have their way.

Let justice put their neighbours down,
But on themselves she must not frown;
Just give them everything they want –
Foul slander, aye, and blazing cant.

These blatant fools would shout aloud,
And cast upon the church a cloud;
They blame the parson, clerk and all,
And cry the church must get a fall.

These are the men our town would blame,
Who strive to mar its noble name;
Just by their narrow – minded soul,
And will not balance up the whole.

Cain and Joab their brothers slew,
Ergo – we must have done it too:
This is the way they judge our town,
And strive to keep its honour down.

W.J.G.

41

This piece appeared in The Bulletin – Markets of Belfast, Ballyclare, Larne and Antrim (Gratis) published in Ballyclare by a local printer on 18 June 1889.

*From the memory of some older residents this title line was followed by: 'And every day's like an Easter Monday.' to complete the couplet.

Greetings

As I was going to Ballyclare
And passing by Rashee
I met a man who drove a cart,
And 'Morrow, boy,' says he.

'Morrow, boy' says I to him,
(The day was passing fine)
And that was all; he went his way,
And I went mine.

Harry Browne (John o' the North)

Harry Browne wrote verses on a range of topics for local newspapers – notably The Larne Times. His verses also appeared in a number of books and other publications and were very popular in East Antrim.

The Masher of Lisnalinchy

I'm the masher of sweet Lisnalinchy,
Ach, sure it was there I was born,
And now I am one of the idols
The sweet countryside does adorn.

Chorus

I'm the masher of sweet Lisnalinchy,
There no one with me can compare,
For miles all around I'm the idol,
From Mossley to old Ballyclare.

It was there to the school my ma sent me,
With an overall jacket and hat.
I winked at the bonnie wee lassies
'Til the master he told me to quat.

Chorus

And now sure soon I 'll be finished,
And a thorough good scholar I am,
I'll be a fine gentleman some day,
A real one and not a mere sham.

Chorus

Frae hame sure I ne'er was far travelled,
But just in this style I may roam
My overall jacket just fits me,
As if from gay Paree I have come.

Chorus

I attend all the fairs and the markets
Bazaars and grand concerts and so,
And I go for nine months of the summer
To the beautiful seaside at Doagh.

Chorus

Traditional Song

The May Fair, Dances and lots of Houzledoo

A typical Ballyclare market or fair scene from the late 19th Century

A large crowd always came into Ballyclare for the annual May Fair especially for the evening festivities and the socialising. Many buses brought folk in from the surrounding districts even from as far away as Antrim and Belfast. There was often confusion and excitement at the end of the evening when the buses filled up to head off for local and distant destinations. One May Fair night just before departure time, an old fellow emerged from John Baird's public house and made his unsteady way to the bus station. He stumbled on to one bus after another in a vain attempt to locate the correct vehicle. Eventually he was led by someone who knew him well and placed in a seat where he promptly fell asleep. A clergyman, sitting at the back of the bus, was appalled at his state and behaviour and as the bus headed off he got up, approached him and, putting his hand gently on his shoulder addressed him, 'My good man, do you not realise that you are on the way to eternal perdition?' Opening one eye the old fellow replied, 'Dang it, am I on the wrong bus again?'

* * *

The May Fair attracted rather shady traders from all over Ulster. They would set up their wares on the back of lorries and extol their quality in loud cries hoping to attract a crowd of prospective customers. One Fair day a particularly aggressive trader was addressing his audience and praising the quality and low prices of the bed linen he was endeavouring to sell. He spied an elderly couple heading for his pitch and shouted out to them, 'Look at this, madam, great value in these new sheets!' The old lady shouted back, 'Luksay, boy, him and me are still haein' quare value in the auld yins.'

* * *

Dancing has always been a popular pastime in Ballyclare. Over the years there have been a variety of dance halls to cater for the craze. These were suited to different classes of clients. One in the Back Road (now Harrier Way) rejoiced under the title of 'The Greasy Pig'. It was not patronised by the upper crust! Another venue in a later period in this area was the British Legion Hall a fearfully small dance hall for the crowds who thronged here on Saturday nights. The gentlemen tended to be jammed in close to the wall in tiers, often four deep with the chaps so crushed that they had their arms pinned to their sides. A celebrated wit in this condition shouted out to his friend standing next to him, 'Hey Wull, would you blow my nose for you're nearer it than I am!'

* * *

The Ballyclare Town Hall was the Mecca for dancers of all types – the upper and the lower orders. The style of dancing and behaviour matched the type of audience on any particular evening. There is no doubt that some of the Saturday night dances could turn out very ugly indeed. Very often it was said, 'They fought all o'er the floor and here and there in an odd corner a wee bit of dancing would break out!'

* * *

On other evenings with a different set of dancers decorum prevailed. A special annual event was the Farmers' Union Ball. Evening dress and polished shoes were much to the fore. There was a custom that after the French Chalk had been scattered on the floor the dancing would begin with the President and his wife taking to the floor. One year the president was Wee Tam, a prize ploughman who it was said could turn a pair of horses and a plough on a half crown. His wife was a rather stout lady, stiff in her movements and not an expert dancer. As the couple progressed somewhat clumsily down the hall it became obvious to the embarrassed audience that Tam, with little jerks of his shoulders and elbows, was endeavouring to turn his partner round at the end of the dance floor. Just when it seemed likely that this manoeuvre would be impossible and Tam's dunts were making little impression on his wife's failure to complete the movement, a voice from the band broke the uneasy silence in the hall, 'Tam, head her o'er to the slap (the doorway) and turn her heid doon the hill! (the stairs).' The embarrassed members found it difficult to stifle a giggle!

* * *

On another occasion at the big Saturday night dance, Jock McConnell the impresario, was approached by a young chap who was obviously a newcomer to these affairs with the query, 'Excuse me, Sir, could you please show me to the toilet?' Now this was the first time Jock had had to deal with such a request. It was well known by locals that there were no such modern arrangements in the Town Hall. However, showing admirable resilience, Jock took the stranger by the elbow, guided him to the front door of the hall and told him, 'Now there you are, Sir – onywhere a'tween here and Doagh.'

* * *

A bit of a fracas had developed at the Saturday night dance in the Town Hall and Wee Wullie, a rough customer, was flailing his way with flying fists up one side of the dance floor. When he reached the stage he was hailed by a bandsman, 'You're in good form, Wull. Where's the brother the night?' Back came the reply, 'He's bringin' up a sward on the ither side.'

Ballyclare Hiring Fair

Come all ye lads and lassies
A while and with me share,
Frolics and come – all – ye's
Of the Ballyclare Hiring Fair.

The market square was filled
With folks of every kind,
Rich and poor, good and bad
The halt, the lame, the blind.

Gypsy Smith in her tent
Would your fortune tell.
The harness man and delph woman
Had many goods to sell.

A favourite was 'Tie the Boy '
Used rope, wire and chains,
And for the folk's enjoyment
Suffered untold pains.

Seated around the monument,
Were men of different age,
Waiting for the farmers
To offer a hiring wage.

The man who drank the paraffin
To his mouth put a light
And out from it came gushing flames,
That gave us all a fright.

There were hard nuts and yellow man
Goldfish and white mice,
And a Crown and Anchor table
Was played with loaded dice.

Young and old danced with joy
In the spacious Market Square,
For this indeed was the climax
Of the Ballyclare Hiring Fair.

The lights were slowly dimming,
The whistle gave a shrill,
Midnight was approaching
It was one minute till.

The amusement lights went slowly out,
Silence filled the air,
Time had brought an ending
To the Ballyclare Hiring Fair.

Alfie McClean

Larne Hiring Fair

Although the following lines describe a hiring Fair in Larne the scene would have been very similar to fairs in Ballyclare.

…………..they come from Ballynure an' Straid,
Frae doon the shore, aye, an' the Braid
Gleno, Raloo an' Islandmagee
Frae Feystown, Mageraban, Rashee.

A' dressed up in their Sunday suits,
They've creeshed their hair an' blacked their boots
Intent for yince tae cut a dash,
An' buy some fun wi' well-earned cash.

There's watches goin' for three an' six,
There's corkscrew knives an' walkin' sticks,
Drinks, apples, nuts an'yellow man
An' spae wives there tae read yer han'.

That's where you'll find the servant girls,
Afore they go in search o'erls
For maybe printed on their han' –
Is some rich han'some dark young man.

This is their day – their faces show it;
They're brave weel-like, an' man they know it.
An' mony a match that's made this day
Is clinched in kirk afore next May.

Guid ploughmen are in big demand,
Tae cowp Cairncastle's heavy lan'
They'll get their keep an' ten poun clear,
An' that's no bad for yin half-year.

An' then there's useful, handy chaps
Sae guid at biggin' dykes an' slaps,
Can milk a coo or feed a pig,
Can swing a scythe or set a rig.

They'll clean the horses, plait their manes,
An' gie a han' at mindin' weans.
Such chaps as these at this Lairne fair
Can get six guineas – less or mair.

Of coorse there's ither thaveless bein's,
Saft harmless, feckless doits – the lea'ins.
They're happy hokin' in a sheugh,
Or dungin' byres or something rugh.

They get a bed, a bite tae eat
A dud o' claes, clogs tae their feet,
An odd half croon frae time tae time
An' this arrangement works oot fine …..

John Clifford

From The Corran – the journal of the Larne and District Folklore Society.

John Clifford, with Ernie Logan, Matt Meharg and Sam Cross, was one of the loyal band of enthusiasts who who formed the backbone of The Larne and District Folklore Society. He had developed a career in local broadcasting and drew on his extensive knowledge and experience of the working practices on farms in local radio programmes. He often related how, as a young man, he himself had been hired as a 'servant man' at hiring fairs.

Fun on the Farm!

A mean-fisted farmer was ashamed of the state of the trousers habitually worn by his hard-working hired servant man. Eventually he could stick this no longer so one day he told him that going about his work with the large hole in the rear end of his trousers brought shame upon him and the entire household. The hard-working chap replied, 'Well I think if I am to work like a horse, I might as well look like one!'

* * *

The diet for hired hands at farms varied from decent if stodgy fare to very skimpy meals. One mean, hard-fisted farmer expected his servant man to exist on a diet exclusively of turnips – turnips for breakfast, dinner, tea and supper. Complaints from the servant man were regularly aired but nothing changed until the farmer heard that the turnip feasts had become the talk of the neighourhood. So he decided he'd have to change the diet for the sake of his good name and reputation. The next day the servant man was astounded to find his dinner consisted of a huge steak. He tucked in heartily but the sight of the fellow devouring this delicious meal and thinking what it had cost complained bitterly, 'Man dear, there's nearly a whole beast there, it will be roaring inside you!' The servant man replied, 'Well, if it does, you can be sure it will not be for the want of turnips!'

* * *

The first introduction of sileage as winter fodder in Ulster took place on a farm near Ballyclare. The son, Bertie, astounded his father, Bertie senior, who watched the progress of the experiment with interest but with mixed emotions and fears of how it might end up. At the weekly Autumn market in Ballyclare he was asked by a farmer neighbour how the pioneering process was progressing. The old man replied curtly, 'Do you know our Bertie has turned our good hay harvest into dung!'

An aged retired farmer was being interviewed on the radio about the changes that had taken place over his lifetime. The broadcaster mentioned the modern practice of going off for a holiday to far distant destinations. He referred to future plans to allow people to book a flight into Space. 'What do you think of this and those people who intend to set off in a spaceship. 'The old fellow thought for a moment then replied, 'They're fand o'ootins, fand o'ootins.'

* * *

Two old farmers on a wee Ferguson tractor were emerging from a field on to the main road. bouncing through the slap. They were deeply engaged in conversation, the driver turned back to engage with his friend holding grimly with both hands on the mudguards. Suddenly there appeared over the brow of a hill heading towards them at speed a two-seater Mercedes sports car. The driver braked furiously but the only way he could avoid ramming the tractor was to enter the field by the opening from which the tractor and the two old fellows had emerged. As the sports car spun round in a circle to allow the driver to get back on to the road the tractor driver shouted to his friend, 'Wullie, aren't we the lucky boys we got out of that field before that edjit went into it!'

The Verses of Jock Gilmour

The Belfast Telegraph edition of Tuesday, 13th December 1938 printed an article by Sam Henry, the celebrated Coleraine folklorist and song collector, on the poetry of Jock Gilmour. The following is an extract taken from this newspaper article. Sam Henry met with drinkers in The Five Corners Inn and asked what they knew about Jock Gilmour. Later he was able to meet and talk with Jock himself at Rashee, Ballyclare.

'On a day I hied me to the Five Corners, Ballyclare and at the inn fireside, I learnt more about the bard. Faces lit up when I mentioned him, and his neighbours were proud to repeat tags of his verses.

Jock was not at home but, foolishly I admit, I went to see the chimney the jackdaw had sat on. Under the guidance of a Rashee farmer I went to see the poet and found him in the act of sawing down a tree. A man of less than ordinary stature and fresh complexion, blue eyes and an expression in them of an optic lens, he was my friend at once because I was able to recite the little poem about the Jackdaw.

He had a slouch, felt hat well pulled down. From beneath it he examined me quizzically to see what underlay my visit. He wrote verse much as a blackbird sings, natural and unrestrained. And he wrote of things he loved. The mood came upon him at times and then the fires died away for months. His volcano of poesy was intermittent.

Love of country, affection for God's creatures, lively humour, gentle satire and brotherly goodwill, these mark the poems of Jock Gilmour of The Five Corners.

That he makes poetry at all is something of a miracle; that his thoughts blossom on the lonely outpost of Dunamoy is stranger still and that one man with a ballad can hold his fellows where the great and mighty fail, shows the wizardry of the poet's dream.'

The Jackda'

Jackda, jackda you cunnin' villain;
I see you're at the chimney fillin';
You hae made the job complete;
Tramped them doon in wi' your feet.

You would nae like it mare nor me,
If you were blin' wi' reek and couldnae see;
I dinnae want to gi' you ony bother,
I doubt you'll hae tae big anither.

You needn't begin tae carry strae
For in that nest you'll nivver lay;
Why don't ye tak' the haunted biggin'
And build some place aboot the riggin'

I cannae get the fire lit;
Some yin o' us 'll hae tae flit;
Seein' you can rise and flee,
Maybe you'll go and let me be.

The Hedgehog

Push your face out of the jags
So that you can see;
Toddle on where'er you're goin';
No need to turn for me.

You may snuff and blink and try to think,
But could you understand,
This place as much belongs to you
As it does to any man.

I suppose you lay and snored and slept,
Till now you have to steal;
If you care to eat a turnip,
You'll get one in the other fiel'.

Maybe you're only out for fun,
Or your mate you're goin' to see.
It will be a jaggy courtin',
When you get her on your knee.

* * *

The story goes that Jock was sitting outside the Five Corners pub
one afternoon when a car stopped and the driver approached
him,'Could you tell me, old man, where do those five roads go?'
Jock replied, 'Weel boy, a dinnae know whur they go during the
nicht but they're always back there in the mornin' again. 'On
another occasion a passing tourist addressed him, 'I dare say you
have lived all your life in this district?' 'No yit!' was Jock's quick
reply.

The Five Corners Pub

On Nature

I pick no flowers; that wins the bee:
The garden mouse comes near to play;
Indeed he turns his eyes away.
Say what you like, all things love me:
Horse, cow, and mouse; bird moth and bee.

The Devil at the Five Corners

At the Corners five, man alive!
The devil did appear;
He passed us by like wind and sky,
And filled our hearts wi' fear.

Some said he'd a pair o' horns,
Others said he had a tail,
For they saw it birlin' roon his heid,
Like the souple o' a flail.

A Verse extolling Nature

What moves that man is when the blind bat taps
His window when he sits alone at night;
Or when the small bird sounds like some great beast
Among the dead dry leaves so frail and light.

**On reaping corn and unfortunate enough to behead a
corncrake, Jock expresses sorrow for the dead bird.**

If I had known you were so near,
I would have chased you out of danger;
It did no good to spill your blood,
O, poor and harmless stranger.

Where you dwell I cannot tell,
Or when you come and go;
You know your book to sling your hook,
Before the frost and snow.

But what's the use of talking now;
Your life I can't restore;
I'll fling the steel right to the de'il,
And I'll mow corn no more.

Tall Tales from the Parish

In the past ordinary country folk often told yarns involving the local clergymen. This did not display an absence of respect – quite the contrary. For their part, the clergy often got their own back when 'performing' at socials and concerts. Many took a pride in telling anecdotes and stories that had been passed down orally in the neighbourhood.

The local minister, walking through Ballynure late on a Saturday night met a member of his congregation obviously the worse for drink following a night in The Ballad Inn. He reprimanded him in a stern voice. 'Oh, drunk again, Tom, drunk again!' He was met by a slurred reply, 'Sure, so am I, your reverence, so am I.'

* * *

On another occasion he was not altogether surprised to meet this congregation member in a similar condition. He reproached him offering the advice, 'Tom, when you are tempted to spend a night in a public house you should say, 'Get thee behind me, Satan.' 'Oh, I do, your reverence, I do, but he gets behind me and pushes me in!'

* * *

Tom eventually took the pledge and for some months he struggled to keep his promise to remain teetotal. Then one Saturday night the minister caught sight of him sneaking out of the pub by the back door. 'Tom ! Tom! Are you not observing the rules of your pledge?' 'Oh yes, but not strictly, your reverence I am now a teetotaller but not a bigoted one!'

* * *

Martha was greeted by the minister at the church door as she left following a particularly long sermon.

'Well, Martha, how did you enjoy this morning's service?

'Weel, Your Reverence,' she replied, 'ye'll hae tae mind yin thing, the heid 'll only tak' in whit the backside'll thole.'

* * *

Often the greatest challenge for a clergyman was visiting members of his congregation living in modest circumstances. Sometimes he would be invited to partake of a meal. On one such visit a minister was offered a bowl of broth. Hesitantly he agreed. The lady of the house set down the bowl of broth and he found it was delicious. While he ate a little dog sidled up to the table, looked hungrily at the bowl of broth and barked excitedly. 'Oh would you just look at that,' said the minister, 'the wee fellow would just love a taste of the broth.'

'Oh, no,' said the hostess, 'it's not the broth he's after, your reverence – you see it's the sight of his wee dinner bowl that's got him so excited!'

* * *

On another occasion as the visiting minister conversed with an elderly member of his congregation he idly helped himself from a bowl of nuts sitting on the kitchen table. The nuts gradually disappeared until there were none left. Rather embarrassed he said he was so sorry to have eaten the whole bowl of nuts.

'Oh don't worry about that Your Reverence. It's not a serious loss, you see, I love those bars of fruit and nut chocolate. I'm not too fond of the nuts so I just spit them out into that little bowl before throwing them into the bin.'

* * *

Domestic rows were important times when ministers were often asked for advice and sometimes proved difficult to settle. One clergyman found a constant visitor to his door was a member of his congregation who insisted that he suffered endlessly from the ravages of his wife's temper.

Said he to the patient minister, 'She's a terror, your reverence. You'll have to come over, see what she's like, speak to her and see what you can do to bring peace to an unhappy home.'

The minister was most reluctant to intervene but the husband insisted and gave such a dreadful picture of these affairs that he eventually agreed to go along with him to see what he could accomplish. As they approached the house, through the back gate the husband instructed the minister,

'Now, your reverence, just you stand there a couple of minutes until I go in and get her started!'

* * *

The clergy were not always at their best when visiting schools to assist in religious education. A minister who had just come to a country congregation from a charge in the city was explaining to the class the story of the good shepherd and the lost sheep. He asked the class why they thought the shepherd had taken so much trouble to rescue this particular sheep from the thicket. There was complete silence until a farmer's son from the back of the room piped up,

'That's easy, Sir. It was the tup.'

The wee chap evidently knew more than the minister about rearing sheep!

* * *

Another time the story of the Prodigal Son was the topic for discussion. At the end of this wonderful story the minister asked the class, 'Now, children, at the feast for the homecoming of the son who had gone astray, who was feeling very unhappy at the celebration?'

He hoped, of course, to hear the answer – the jealous brother. But instead a little girl shouted out, 'The fatted calf, Sir.'

* * *

A new furniture shop opened in Ballyclare and soon was doing excellent business. Nothing was known about the owner, a stranger to the town. The clergy naturally were anxious to discover which religious denomination he belonged to. With no information on this vital matter forthcoming the ministers from the Presbyterian Church, the Church of Ireland, the Methodist Church and the Parish Priest met together one morning and drew up a cunning plan. They would all go down the street together, stand outside the premises and go into the shop in turn, engage the owner in general conversation and with subtle questions draw out the information they required. The Presbyterian minister went in first and came out to say, 'No further on lads, but I must admit he is an excellent salesman. He has just sold me a new wardrobe. ' The Methodist and the Church of Ireland ministers fared no better with obtaining the information they sought but each was persuaded to make purchases – a new dressing table for one and an expensive china cabinet for the other. The Parish Priest felt he would do no better than his colleagues but headed into the shop anyway. In a few minutes he was back and said to his colleagues,

'Well, lads I still do not know what denomination he is but I can tell you this confidently. He is definitely not one of ours – he tried to sell me a double bed!'

* * *

Wee Maggie, a life long spinster, lived on her own in a small cottage with a large garden where she kept a flock of chickens. The minister visited her one afternoon and was intrigued by the chickens which were all singing happily as they pecked the grains of corn thrown out by Maggie. 'That's a grand flock, Maggie, but tell me, you have a dozen hens there but why do you need three roosters?'

'Well, your reverence, don't I know what it's like to be neglected!'

When Aliens Landed in Doagh

When the aliens landed in Doagh, by
They must a geen them a fright.
Now they werene there afore bedtime
They must a come down in the night.

I was takin' a walk wey the dog, hey
When I seen this big round UFO
I shouts, 'Cum on out an' see us
Us Doagh yins won't hurt ye, ye know.

The locals they cum out tey see it,
This odd and peculiar craft.
'Hey, Jimmy, they'll gee us a sail now'
'Och, Hughie don't be so daft!'

The big lights cum on right above us
Like the Christmas Tree down in The Square.
An a door opened just as if magic
An my wee dug he ran like a hare.

Then two or three tiny wee figures
Cum out an they stood on the steps
By, they werenae the height o' two daisies
But we stepped back and took off our ceps.

They'd cum here to learn o' our lingo,
An te improve their accent as well
Seys I, 'Now ye've cum te the right place
For in Doagh we speak clear as a bell'

The Heed Yin he waved his wee finger,
He's like thon E.T. only blue
Seys he 'Would you like to see inside?'
Seys I, 'Can Big Jimmy cum too?'

Now we didnae need te be asked twice
We dashed up the stair in a jif,
The big door it closed right behind us
An the Heed Yin seys 'Watch while we lift'

Off the ground like a Hallowe'en rocket,
We sailed away up past the stars.
An we started right into yon project
To make 'Doagh – speak' the language o' Mars.

We talked and we chatted and yarned, by,
On our intergalactical trip.
The wee yins they seemed nice and friendly
An they didnae gie 'any auld lip'

The Heed Yin he offered us dinner
An I seys 'Thanks all the same,
But if it's all right with you Mars Yins
I think that I'd rather go hame.'

Now Jimmy, he was all affronted
At me just for makin so bold,
An he seys te me 'Hughie just sit there
An try an just do as yer told.'

But me mind had been made up for definite,
I was missin' me dug an me tay.
Doagh's inter-planetary relations
Had gone far enough for one day.

So we landed in Doagh near the pub, hey,
I was glad but Big Jimmy seys 'No,
I think I'll stay wey the Blue Yins
To teach them to speak right, 'an so,

We shook hans and they prepared take – off
Goodbye Jimmy and Big UFO,
An the blue yin shouts down te us Doagh bys
'Us Mars Yins won't hurt him…Ye know.'

Matthew Gray

*The verses appeared in the Ballyclare High School Magazine in
1997. The composition and recitation won
16-year-old Matthew the title of The Bard of Armagh at the
competition for the best recitation of a traditional ballad.*

Matthew Gray as a pupil at
Ballyclare High School

The Aliens Arrival in Doagh

Leila (Age 7)

In this picture two boys named Jimmy and Hughie are walking their dog. Above them two naughty children are climbing the war memorial while a man with a mohawk is shouting at them to get down. There is a red car with a mummy driving and her son with his hands and nose against the window, and his nose looks like a pig's nose because of that.

There is a paper factory and in the windows there is some kindling, a cardboard box with paper in, stacks of paper, a paper machine and some people.

Next to the paper factory door there is a girl riding her bike, next to the bike riding girl there is the man about to cross the road, above the car there are two pretty girls with their mum on the way to school.

Above the paper factory there is a UFO carrying three little aliens.

Zoe (Age 6)

The Stick-Men of Burnside

Down by Burnside's 'showrye ' banks, there is an old Scutch mill,
For cleaning tow and scutching flax, they always get their fill.
The other day I passed this way there was a funny sound
In Barklie's fiel' I saw the wheel of a cart turned upside down.
I enquired who the driver was, I asked old Jock McGrugan,
He said it was a young lad by the name of Jackie Coogan.
I heard a saw then murmuring as I headed for Kilbride,
From the pub the noise was coming, 'twas the Stick-Men from Burnside.

We must salute these gentlemen for they have hard to work
For they're the boys can do it, the sons of Harry Turk.
A word of praise I give to them especially Frank and Yunk
For we never want a fire now except when they get drunk.
Harry has got an Austin 10, it needs a good rebore,
When the neighbours see him coming they run in and shut the door!
Sure when he gets her going well he'll feel a different man
When he's sailing round by Cushendall along with Mary Ann.

Now, Harry, just be careful let 'caution be your guide'
And bring her safely back again to the village of Burnside.

William Hugh Topping

The Darlin' Boy

If upon the road at night
You meet the darlin' Boy,
A bullock or a heifer
He's wallopin' wi' joy.

He'll stop with all his neighbours
And he'll yarn a while with you.
The only fault the darlin' has
Is drinking Mountain Dew.

He'll rise up in the morning
An' gie his e'en a rub,
Then off to auctions, fairs or markets
Or else it's into a pub.

He'll sit and tell to Davie
His daelin' tricks galore
And how he bought the black yin
The best yin o' the score.

He'll rise an' go tae the market
The Dookers they'll go too,
A pair o' as able dodgers
As ever driv' a coo.

Tam brings up the black yin
And Jim brings up the rear,
Then says Dealer Wullie
We'll hae tae persevere.

The Darling Boy lived at Kilbride. He enlisted in the 12th Battalion of The Royal Ulster Rifles and was killed on 1st July 1916 on the Somme. The Dookers were his two brothers. It is not known who wrote the lines.

Cogry Mill

Oh, Cogry Mill, why keep so still
Through years of deep depression ?
It now appears since you closed down
Six years have made completion.

The poor do wait in idle state,
How dark is their tomorrow,
But may you have some thought in store
To lift their veil of sorrow.

We can't deny in days gone by
Your works were never ceasing,
Your hopes were high, your prospects good
Your hands were aye increasing.

I hope, through time, you'll change your mind,
This is my fond wish spoken;
Give idle work, unite again
The links that you have broken.

L. A. O'Neill
Hollybank, Templepatrick (1923)

Cogry Square

Cogry Cinema

'It was a real treat in those days to go to see the pictures in Cogry Cinema. The story goes about a chap (I knew him as he sang in the church choir in Parkgate of which I too was a member) that he met a girl one evening and decided to take her to Cogry Picture House. They stood in the queue for a while and as they moved up to the door he 'nudged' his girlfriend and said, 'Give me your shilling and I'll pay for the both of us.' (A shilling was the price of admission in those days.)

Nancy Wilson
Kilbride

(who enjoyed an evening at the pictures in Cogry)

Cogry Mill and the Liverpool Boat

Some years ago Cogry Spinning Mill needed to find a replacement for their man who served as a Stoker / Engineer. It proved difficult to recruit an experienced hand for the important position but eventually the manager decided he had found a competent employee and he was hired. All that was known about him was that, though he was a bit long in the tooth, he had served in roughly this role for thirty years on the Belfast to Liverpool steamship ferry.

The new chap settled in quite happily and for a time things went very smoothly in the mill's engine room. It was noted, however, that he had a habit on a Friday of spending his lunch time in Alex Toppings' pub, just up the road from the works. It was also noted that sometimes he was not too punctual on his return to duty. On a particular Friday he was seen not only to be very late on return but struggling to hold a straight line walking along towards the entrance to the mill. About an hour after his return huge billows of smoke were seen pouring out of the chimney and the wheels driving the spinning machinery began to rotate furiously with the spinning frames almost jumping out of their fixings. The noise in the main building was deafening and the manager was so concerned that he sent over to the owner's residence to implore him to come over and find out what was happening. Mr McMeekin arrived at the engine room in a panic only to be greeted by the rather inarticulate engineer with a smile of satisfaction on his purple face announcing, 'Now don't you worry about a thing, captain. I have everything under control and I'll have her safely at the quay in Liverpool dead on time!'

Story attributed to Jack Gowdy

Tinker Graham and 'Gouldie'

Gouldie Graham was an infamous Ballyclare character. His father was a tinker who travelled round the local farms repairing tin cans. Often he was not greeted with enthusiasm but he had acquired a particular skill in arriving suddenly at farmhouse back doors. Ballyclare folk boasted he could, 'Walk through the hale o' Egypt and no a dug wudda barked at him.' Gouldie joined up in the First World War and quickly acquired the reputation of being 'the laziest soldier in the British army' passing a low threshold indeed. One time, while home on leave, he had his father make him a special tin can. The circumference of the can was just a little bit wider than the official tin cans issued to the troops. Thereafter the brigade commander couldn't understand why the rum ration did not go as far as usual!

* * *

When a few locals got together and decided to form a flute band sometime around the 1920s they sent one of their number, not the brightest spark in the group, off to Belfast to purchase some instruments. There he addressed the sales assistant, 'A wud like two' r 'thee flutes.' The salesman replied 'Certainly, Sir, which do you require, sharp or flat?' Pausing for a moment, the prospective flute player stammered, 'Och! just them wee roon yins like all the ithers.'

Snippets from the Second World War

The Collin Crash

It was early here one morning
Before the break of day,
A Yankee Liberator crashed
Upon the Collin brae.

It's a heathered part of Ireland,
Where you smell the heather bloom.
A place we never want to see
Another bomber comin' doon.

The people in the district
Got up, some ran half clad,
To give First Aid as Britons would
To these dying Air Force lads.

We mourn the loss of these great men
That flew through thick and thin,
To blast and bomb to pieces
That big city of Berlin.

With a ring of steel around them now
Every German town they'd smash,
Where they're making soup from cabbage
Hitler grew from human ash!

When this war is over
It's up to our 'Big Three'
To plant in the heart of Germany
A true democracy.

Anon

A Page from Sandy Robinson's Diary
for Sunday 23 February 1941

Snow about two inches deep. Some places heavy frost. Big Sam Wilson dead.

Mother sitting in the parlour feeling better after bad cold.

Jack is sitting by the fireside reading the Bible – half an hour ago he got his finger cut badly as he was letting out the bull.

Father sitting at opposite side of the fire looking at picture book – namely 'Illustrated'.

Jeannie is sitting beside me looking over a book entitled The British Gospel Trumpet. The wireless is tearing away, there's a sort of Treasure Island play on.

Robert is shaving.

The time is now 4.32pm. The canaries are singing and a hen must have laid an egg by the noise she's making. Eggs are 1/6 per pound. There are usually eight in a pound.

The kettle is boiling for tea – we don't know what we will have to eat but we know what we won't have – onions, bananas, jam, sugar, cheese.

The Germans are about to march into Bulgaria. A British pilot has just shot down six Italian planes.

Kilbride Platoon Home Guard marching through Doagh

Included in the above photo: Captain Jack Ross, leading his men.

1st Row, second from right – Ben Todd
2nd Row, extreme left – Will Todd
3rd Row, extreme right – Davy Moore
4th Row, extreme right – Willie Warwick
6th Row, second left – Joe Montgomery

Leader of the second group – James Spence
2nd Row, extreme left – Andy Wilson
2nd Row, second from left – Billy Strange
6th Row, second from left – Billy Gault
7th Row, extreme left – Tom Leitch

* * *

It was a terribly wet and stormy night as the local platoon of the Local Defence Volunteers, the forerunners of the Home Guard, met in the village hall on their normal Parade Night. This evening the topic for discussion was an issue raised at every meeting – the lack of a proper supply of rifles for the platoon. They felt that the substitutes of brush shafts and agricultural implements did not fit in with the dignity of the unit. On this evening, Harry, not the most articulate of members, volunteered to make his way through the wind and rain to the telephone box in the village and contact Headquarters in Lisburn and take up the matter of the missing guns. Soaked to the skin and in a foul mood, he put his four pennies into the slot on the coin box and eventually a senior colonel answered and demanded to hear about his problem. The line was poor and the colonel quickly became frustrated as he failed to grasp the gist of what Harry was saying. He abruptly shouted down the line 'What are you talking about? Speak up, man. Buns! Do you expect me to send your chaps buns? Talk sense man, stop dithering!' Harry, dripping from head to toe, lost his cool and bellowed down the line, 'Lucksay, it's not Buns, I'm referring to, it's Guns. I will spell it out for you. G-U – for God and Ulster for whom we are fighting, N for pneumonia and, if I have to stand here much longer, I'm sure to get it, and S for civility of which I have to say, Sir, you have got damned little!'

The angry colonel was quick to replace his receiver!

* * *

The Second World War broke out on a very hot Sunday in September 1939. A resident from Ballynure listened to the ominous news on the wireless. Later that morning he was riding his bicycle up towards Ballyeaston and, looking over the hedge, spied a friend out in the field checking up on his cattle – a typical Sunday duty. He hailed him,

'John, I just heard on the wireless that war has been declared and the Germans have marched into Poland.' Back came the reply,

'And a grand day they have got for it too!'

The 1940s brought increasing mechanisation on the farm

Tam Wilson's Tractor

In Ballinashie near Ballyclare of high renown and fame,
There lives a quiet young farmer, Tam Wilson is his name,
He drives a converted tractor – she is by make a Dodge
She never does refuse to start for her plugs are made by Lodge.

Tam drives her on like fury all records he has broke,
And at times he gets enveloped in a great big cloud of smoke.
And though she has disadvantages for fields that are too small,
Yet what could be done without her I do not know at all.

It's only very seldom that he puts her into low
She's the most infernal puller and she runs on TVO,
The braking system is complete on both the front and rear,
And proudly Tam sticks out his tongue as he shoves her into gear!

There's Hollinger with his Austin and a Ferguson has Willie Rea,
They think they have got the good machines
    but they never saw the day
They could beat the Dodge at pullin' in the fields and on the road,
For boy she is the lady that can shift the heavy load!

There's Kernohan with his David Brown – she is very fast in top,
But compared with Wilson's famous Dodge
    she's only a bunch o' scrap.
And then comes Gardiner's Fordson,
    it's well known she has the power,
But she never was built to travel at forty miles an hour.

So, come all you local farmers now,
    you have heard what I have said
You till the land with tractors where your fathers used the spade,
Just put your hands together and with me you will agree
There's none to beat this famous Dodge for miles round
    Ballinashie.

Robert J Hollinger

Bob Hollinger farmed at Carnalee a few miles north of Ballyclare. He had a lively interest in the history and cultural background of the Ballyvoy, Carnanee and Tildarg townlands. In his later years he was an enthusiastic member of the Ballyclare and District Historical Society.

*The following verse appeared in The Newsletter
sent in by Robert Hollinger*

The Irish Moilie O

Old Ireland once had splendid cows,
Her own peculiar breed.
And healthy, hardy cows were they,
That thrived on poorest feed.
At smallest cost, with little care,
They made the rich milk flow;
The peasant lived, his children thrived,
On Irish Moilie O.

But Scotsmen came to Dublin town,
Alas for Ireland then!
They banned and barred our native cow
These strong and ruthless men.
They introduced their fancy breeds,
Till every cattle show
Proclaimed them champions and despised
Our Irish Moilie O.

A Lass o' the Misty Burn

Is it me that knows Glenwherry?
Aye every twist and turn,
For there I courted when I was young
The lass of the Misty Burn.

Her eyes were as blue as the lint,
Her step was light and free;
And of all the lads who shared her smiles,
She kept her heart for me.

Is it me that knows Glenwherry?
Aye every bush on the brae,
For there we wandered by stream and stone
The lee – long summer day.

The flowers that blossomed on the lanes
They bloomed for her and me.
O, merry the world when the heart is young,
And the blackbird sings on the tree.

Is it me that knows Glenwherry?
Aye every blade of grass
That decks the grave on the Collin side,
Where sleeps my ain true lass.

The elm's soft shoots have sprung again,
And green the frond on the fern;
But sad is the song that the blackbird sings,
By the banks o' the Misty Burn.

John o' the North (Harry Browne)

Sandy Robinson, fondly known as The Bard of Ballyalbanagh

Sandy Robinson hailed from Ballyalbanagh where his family have farmed for generations. He achieved renown as someone who had an ability to indulge in amusing and sharp repartee in conversation with acquaintances and in the verses and ballads he composed. The best known of these, and still recited locally, is one he wrote about the Ballyclare Town Hall following its renovation in the 1930s.

His repertoire was extensive but the verses were written on scraps of paper and shoved haphazardly in a cupboard. In 1983 his niece, Joanne Robinson, managed to collect a large number of these and arrange to have them published in a book entitled The Bard of Ballyalbanagh that circulated locally and to great acclaim.

Sandy had an amazing gift for original and appropriate language which comes through in his verses. He had also an encyclopedic knowledge of the Bible from which he could quote at will.

He worked for a time as a butcher with his brother, Jack, in Ballyclare and Carrickfergus and as a builder on a variety of jobs around local farms. It is known that at least one farmer used to think up jobs for Sandy to do on his farm just to have the pleasure of listening to his wisecracks at the tea breaks.

Essentially, however, he was a shy, retiring person and never seemed happy to recite his ballads on stage. In the 1940s /1950s he did contribute to a radio broadcast about The Christmas Rhymers and their unannounced visits to farms and houses in the Ballyboley district. He did appear in public on stage as a member of various musical groups playing the accordion or fiddle. He was also an enthusiastic member of Ballyboley Pipe Band for many years.

The subjects of his verses varied from those of an amusing nature to a compassionate and sensitive approach to characters and episodes.

Sandy's and his dear wife, Jean's headstone in Rashee Cemetery contains a couplet from one of his verses:

> *'The flowers, the sunsets, the tints on a tree,*
> *Were glimpses of heaven to Jeannie and me.'*

A perfect image of Sandy – the poet and the man.

Sandy's Stories

Sandy Robinson was noted and admired for his witty remarks and anecdotes. He always had the quick retort for every occasion. For some years he had a butcher's shop in the North End of Ballyclare. One morning an old lady shuffled into the shop ready to argue with him over the issue of the wrong change he had given to her the previous day.

'Mr Robinson,' she began, 'I have a complaint!'

Quick as a flash Sandy replied,

'Do you know I have often wondered why you walked like that.'

Later Sandy moved into the building trade where he readily found work on local farm premises. On one farm the lady of the house brought him his ten o'clock cup of tea. Sandy preferred good strong tea and this particular cup of tea was much too weak for his liking. As he began to drink the lady appeared with a jug of hot water saying,

'Mr Robinson, that tea may be too strong for you, perhaps you would prefer a drop of water in it?'

'No missus, but here, if that water is any stronger, put it in!'

* * *

He was working on a faulty kitchen sink outlet one morning when the farmer's wife came out and offered to make him a cup of tea. He gladly accepted the offer but got on with the job. In a few minutes he was drenched by a stream of water issuing from the sink outlet pipe. The lady had rinsed out the teapot forgetting that the sink had been disconnected by Sandy. She rushed out apologising profusely to Sandy standing beside the outlet in his sodden dungarees. Grinning he quipped,

'Do you know, I didn't think you would be so quick with the tea!'

* * *

Occasionally, but not too often, some people got the better of him with their sharp remarks. He was looking round the farmyard on a job one day and the farmer's wife, a noted wit herself, asked,

'Sandy, what's up?'

'Aggie, A hae loost the hemmer.'

'Oh don't worry yersel' Sandy, it'll eventually turn up.' Pausing a moment she added,

'On the bill, Sandy, on the bill!'

The Highway Code, the Sawmill Road and Jamie's Houdan Hen

There's lights and signs and long white lines at crossin's, braes and bends
To chart the path where sudden death occasionally descends,
And yet there's fools who spurn the rules – like dames and drunken men,
But the curse that's worse to Safety First is Jamie's Houdan hen.

She'll give her rough oul muff a cuff and strut across the road
With no respect in fact, for acts, much less the Highway Code.
You brake, you swerve, you lose your nerve and nine times oot o' ten
You'll shear a gear by steerin' clear o' Jamie's Houdan hen!

She jumps and haps through gaps and slaps, tae fill ye fu' o' fear,
The rips and squeals o' brakes and wheels is music tae her ear,
There's no' a source, a cause or force ootside the Devil's Den
That scrapes or skins mair knees and shins than Jamie's Houdan hen.

She seldom feeds on fleas and seeds, or luks for pritta moul',
Tae hump and kick and claw and pick, like ony ither fowl,
Instead she sits and dabs her hips, tae somethin' comes – and then –
A desperate dash, another crash for Jamie's Houdan hen.

Wee Sam Magee from Ball'nashee was passin' on his bike
An' goin' at speed – she knocked him heid an' shouthers thro' a dyke,
Now left wi' scars where handlebars had gored his abdomen
He blames the code, Sawmill road, and Jamie's Houdan hen.

A hae run o'er ducks an cats an pups, fell off an' tore m' coat,
An' lost m' share o' skin an' hair collidin' wi' a goat.
I've kicked the lugs o' bitin' dugs, frae Kells tae Killyglen,
But I never met a terror yet like Jamie's Houdan hen.

There's folk in splints, wi' limps an' squints, a sorry sight to see,
An' some got thumps that given them lumps where hollows used to be,
Tho' blid's been spilt there's nane been kil't but Heaven knows just when
Your journey's end could yet depend on Jamie's Houdan hen.

Sandy Robinson

Strangers to the Ballyclare district often struggled to understand the Ulster-Scots language of the area. A locum doctor in the Ballynure practice experienced many difficulties when he arrived from Belfast but he prided himself on how he managed to cope and treat his patients. However one afternoon he found himself beaten by the speech of an elderly patient.

Eventually he had to interrupt the consultation to confer with his colleague in the next room. He began thus, 'I thought I had mastered the dialect. I now recognise and understand words like – heid, fit, thrapple, lugs and oxter – but that old lady in there has me completely baffled.'

'What did she refer to?' asked his colleague.
'Her Yit.'
'That's a new one on me, what was the context?'

'Well, she told me she was riding her bike down the Yett Brae in Ballyalbanagh, a hen ran across the road and she ran straight into the thorn dike. 'And do you know, Doctor,' she said, 'the thorns are in me yit!'

The Killin' o' the Pig

True Byoo wuz comin fae Raloo
The nakht he kallt McCaamont's soo.
He hut her fair between the een –
The cleanest clout ye avver seen.
Whun doon she went withoot a squeal
The oul collie dug wuz at her heel.
He turned aboot an lot a yell
An in the gate he run lik hell.

McCaamont heerd the noise an fuss,
Lukkt ower the waw an seen the bus.
Then oot he cam tae hae a squaat,
Says he 'Boy, whut made you dae thaat?
True Byoo says: 'Maan can ye no see,
Yer pig ran oot in frunt o me?
Fur on ma brake an clutch a stuid
But that aw proved tae be nae guid'

Then the poaliss cum up fae oot the toon
An they mazhured the road baith up an doon.
Yin poalissman tae the ither saes:
'Nae mair on this roadside she'll graze'

The owner's son says 'Aa heerd a whid –
Allooed the soo wuz wurrth fifteen quid'
But his brither says 'Ye'r makin fun,
That soo wuz weel wurrth thurrty pun!'

Then the soo wuz tukk tae the abatwaur,
An buttshers cum fae the Lord knows whaur.
Each there in his greedy sowl,
Tae buy the pig chaep that wuz noo stane – coul.

Weel the buttsher at baukht the soo, they say,
He wunnered whut he'd better dae
Fur the clout she got, the soo t'would spoil,
'Whut diznae dae tae fry' says he 't'wull mebby dae tae boil'

So he made some intae sausage meat;
Her heid, her lugs an aw her feet.
Whut wudnae sell as sausage meat, he sore he'd ca' it veal.
Aa'll tell ye hoo he ended up – he only loast the squeal!

Thomas Hugh Robinson (Larne)
Edited by R. G Gregg c.1950

Robert J Gregg was Professor Emeritus of Linguistics at the University of British Columbia. He was born in Larne in 1912 and grew up when Ulster-Scots was a living language in East Antrim. He first attended Queen's University, Belfast then was awarded his doctoral degree at the University of Edinburgh on the subject 'The Boundaries of the Scotch-Irish Dialects in Ulster'. For many years this was a standard reference for scholars.

He was the first President of The Ulster-Scots Language Society in the 1980s and was a most enthusiastic supporter of the work of the society. Though resident in Canada at this time he regularly sent to the Society copies of local poems and recitations from East Antrim. These used his revised spelling system for Ulster-Scots.

The Kaillin o the Soo included above is an example of this system in practice.

The Relief of Ballyclare

On Tuesday 21 November 1989, Ballyclare was relieved by a company of Engineers from City Mechanical Services who installed a public toilet in the Market Square, a convenience that the patient people of this town had awaited since their Urban Council laid the first plans for such a facility in 1937.

This auspicious occasion must merit some
　　verse with perhaps a refrain,
Telling how it arrived on a lorry, then
　　was gently let down by a crane:
The place was hardly deserted,
　　but at first not a soul turned a hair,
So with very little commotion,
　　the apparatus arrived in the Square.

Eventually the workmen got started,
　　the drills and the hammers drummed,
By twenty – to – five it was over –
　　Ballyclare's Superloo had been plumbed.
Long before this the locals got curious,
　　they couldn't understand it at all,
Was it just a wee house for controlling
　　the parking around the Town Hall?
Well you wouldn't have believed the reaction
　　as news spread like fire round the town,

There had never been such an attraction
    since the Cunningham Monument came down,
Indeed, by half-five at the railings,
    a long queue was starting to form.
And this at the time of the evening
    when tea or the pub was the norm!

At the head of this line stood an old man,
    who with both hands, was wiping his tears,
'I have lived all my life round in Park Street
    and have waited for this day for years.'
The Ballyclare Council once argued
    where the site of new toilets might be
But the lack of the finance delivered
    a K.O. to their planned W.C.

Had the Loo been officially opened –
    and it surely deserved a big fuss,
They'd have come from the district to see it –
    from Doagh and Burnside on the bus!
But the Council are tight with their money –
    they'd never have sanctioned the cash,
Still it's well known on council committees
    that Geordie enjoys a big splash!

The Mayor could have drawn back in splendour
    a curtain of rich velvet plush,
And the councillors await while he entered
    then politely applaud the first flush,
With Victoria band in attendance
    an occasion they wouldn't have missed,
Playing Water Music by Handel
    or even some nice Brahams and Lizst.
That was surely the right way to launch it
    and get the loo off with a birl,

Ballyclare's contribution to Europe –
    its business done 'a la Clochemerle,'
But one can hear the Town Clerk at the council,
    as the figures for sewage he relates,
Claiming spending on toilets as pure waste
    and a terrible drain on the rates.

'They'll soon want more loos round the borough,
    folk must realise that we care
And we'll try to provide several others
    though there isn't the money to spare,
They'll be looking for toilets in Rathcoole,
    at Whiteabbey, Kings Bog and Kilbride
And we're sure to receive a petition
    from golfers for one at Backside.'

But the members stood up for their toilet,
    the compliments flew thick and fast,
A confidence vote was then called for
    and the motion unanimously passed,
The Loo had united the chamber
    and converted the noes into yes
D.U.P., O.U.P. and Alliance in agreement
    and flushed with success!

So it looks like the loo will be staying –
    very much to the locals' relief,
And I bet that its tunes will be playing
    when the one at the bridge comes to grief.
As for me, though I hymn the occasion,
    I will sit down and just rest my case,
'Till the annual May Fair invasion –
    to see if their loo sticks the pace.

Jack McKinney, December 1989

Ballyclare Paper Mill

Only a Memory was composed in 1950 when the Paper Mill closed. This industrial disaster was calamitous for employment in Ballyclare. At the time a verse demonstrating the strong feeling of folk in the town circulated widely.

No more wash – ups no more changes,
No more drinking pints in Grange's
And when our bellies they need filling,
We will think of R.D. Pilling!

R.D. Pilling was the director of the English company that owned the mill and regarded locally as the official responsible for its closure.

Only a Memory

When I gave up smoking,
The old mill chimney said,
They drained my great big boilers,
It really was no thrill,
To feel my bricks get cooler
In winter's frosty chill.

They left me standing useless,
Viewed by the country round;
No smoky, dirty washings
In Ballyclare were found.
Oh ! what a weary sadness
To think my work is done;
I'm just a bleak reminder
Of days all past and gone.

Some people think I'm lovely,
And some would see me down;
But one thing is for certain
This is a poorer town.
For when they write the annals
Of dear old Ballyclare,
They'll mind the paper makers,
And work that once was there.

Rev. L. S. Reid

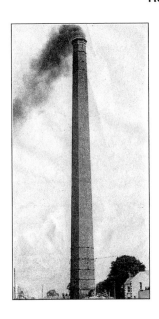 

The tall Mill Chimney was finally demolished by Fred Dibnah from Bolton in 1987. Very little trace of this fine industrial enterprise now remains on the Mill Road site or in the memories of many Ballyclare residents.

An Exile's Tribute to Ballyclare

I've known the Spring in England
And Oh 'tis pleasant there,
When all the buds are breaking
And all the land is fair;
But all the time the heart of me,
The better sweeter part of me
Was sobbin' for the robin
In the Fields o' Ballyclare.

I've known the Spring in England
And Oh 'tis England fair;
With Spring time in her beauty
A queen beyond compare;
But all the time the soul of me
Beyond the poor control of me,
Was sighin' to be flyin'
To the fields o' Ballyclare.

I've known the Spring in England
And now I know it here,
This many a month I've longed for
The openin' of the year;
But oh the Irish mind of me,
(I hope 'tis not unkind of me!)
Is turnin' back the yearnin'
To the fields o' Ballyclare.

Anon

Bibliography

Ye Olde Ballyclarians;   Alfred McClean c.1980

Collection of Poetry by Sandy Robinson
                    Joanne Robinson 1992

The Corran, Larne & District Folklore Society
                    Various editions from 1970

Poems of John Clifford (1900-1983)
                    Larne & District Folklore Society c.1984

Ullans – The Magazine for Ulster-Scots
            The Ulster-Scots Language Society, No 2 Spring 1994

Where the Six Mile Water Flows; Jack McKinney
                    Friars Bush Press 1991

On the Banks of the Ollar – Manuscript history of Ballyclare & District
                    R.T. Grange c.1960-1980

Other Books by Jack McKinney

Facts Figures and Fractions (First Edition) 1980
Facts Figures and Fractions (Second Edition) 1983
They Came in Cars and Carts 1989
Published by The North Eastern Education &
Library Board Area Resources Centre Antrim

Ulster Images: A Cultural Heritage Miscellany
(With Cahal Dallat) 1992
Published by Educational Company, Belfast

Where the Six Mile Water Flows 1990
Published by Friar's Bush Press, Belfast

The Kennedys of Skilganaban, A Family Memoir 2018
Published by Shanway Press, Belfast

Stories of a Lifetime, A memoir of life in Ballyearl, Mossley,
Abbots Cross and Ballyclare 2021
Published by Shanway Press, Belfast